ROSANNE CASH
THE RIVER & THE THREAD

PIANO
VOCAL
GUITAR

3   A FEATHER'S NOT A BIRD

8   THE SUNKEN LANDS

12   ETTA'S TUNE

18   MODERN BLUE

23   TELL HEAVEN

26   THE LONG WAY HOME

29   WORLD OF STRANGE DESIGN

34   NIGHT SCHOOL

37   50,000 WATTS

40   WHEN THE MASTER CALLS THE ROLL

45   MONEY ROAD

ISBN 978-1-4950-6569-9

HAL•LEONARD®
CORPORATION
7777 W. BLUEMOUND RD. P.O. BOX 13819 MILWAUKEE, WI 53213

In Australia Contact:
Hal Leonard Australia Pty. Ltd.
4 Lentara Court
Cheltenham, Victoria, 3192 Australia
Email: ausadmin@halleonard.com.au

Visit Hal Leonard Online at
www.halleonard.com

ROSANNE CASH

The River & the Thread is the 13th studio album by Rosanne Cash and was released in 2014 by Blue Note Records. The critically acclaimed album won 3 Grammy Awards on February 8, 2015. The album swept all the categories that it was nominated for: Best Americana Album, Best American Roots Song and Best American Roots Performance for "A Feather's Not A Bird".

Rosanne Cash has had 11 #1 singles in her career, navigating her own path between country and rock, roots and pop. In 1996, she published a collection of short stories called *Bodies of Water* and in 2000 a children's book: *Penelope Jane: A Fairy's Tale*. Her essays and fiction have appeared in various collections and publications including the *New York Times, Rolling Stone, Time Magazine, The Oxford American,* and *New York Magazine*. In 2010, Viking released Cash's much anticipated memoir, *Composed*, which made the NY Times Bestseller list the first week of release. Rosanne was the recipient of one of the nation's highest songwriting achievements when she was inducted into the Nashville Songwriters Hall of Fame on October 11, 2015. Since 1970, the hall has enshrined some of the greatest writers ever to put words to music including: Willie Nelson, Loretta Lynn, Johnny Cash, Hank Williams, Dolly Parton, Don & Phil Everly, and Roy Orbison just to name a few. Johnny and Rosanne Cash made history as the first father-daughter duo to be inducted to the Hall of Fame.

A FEATHER'S NOT A BIRD

Words and Music by ROSANNE CASH
and JOHN LEVENTHAL

Vocal line written one octave higher than sung.

drive on through to Mem - phis, past ____ the strong-est shoals.
mon-ey's all in Nash - ville, but the lights in - side my head.

Then on to Ar - kan - sas just to touch the gum - bo soul.
So, I'm go - in' down to Flo - rence just to learn to love the thread.

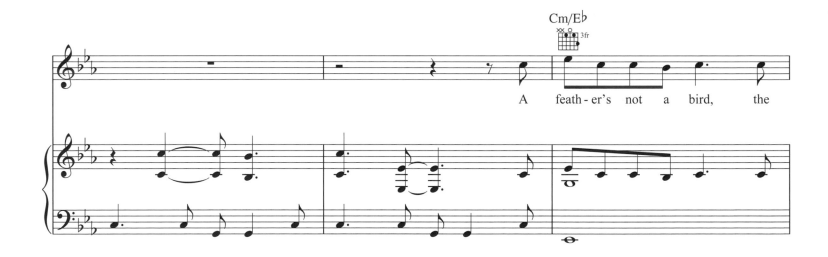

Cm/E♭

A feath-er's not a bird, the

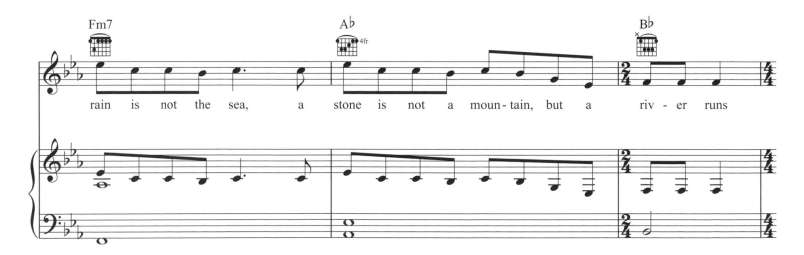

Fm7   A♭   B♭

rain is not the sea, a stone is not a moun - tain, but a riv - er runs

through me.

There's

through me.

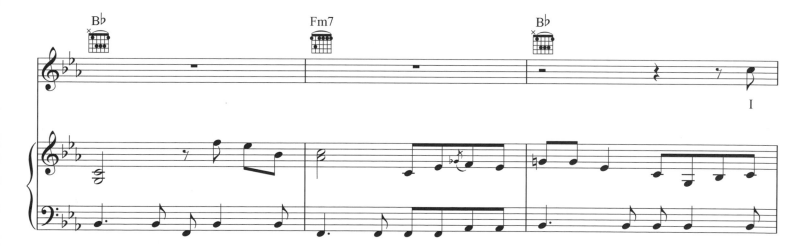

I

burned up sev - en lives and I used up all my charms.

I took the long way home just to end up in your arms.

Cm

That's why I'm go - in' down to Flo - rence, now I got my pret - ty dress.

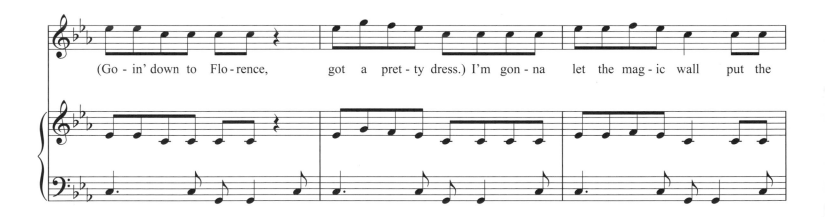

(Go - in' down to Flo - rence, got a pret - ty dress.) I'm gon - na let the mag - ic wall put the

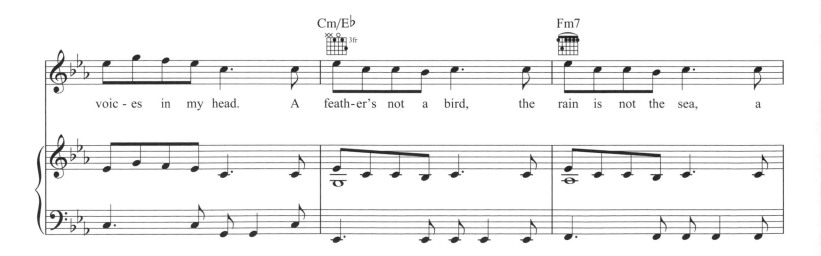

Cm/Eb   Fm7

voic - es in my head. A feath-er's not a bird, the rain is not the sea, a

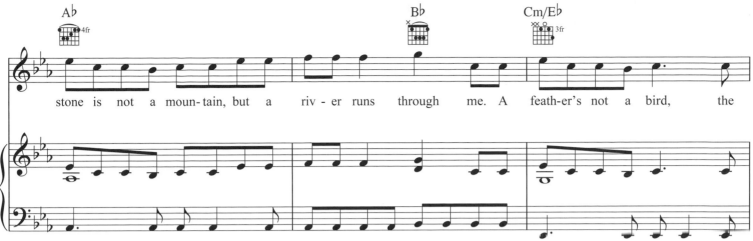

stone is not a moun-tain, but a riv-er runs through me. A feath-er's not a bird, the

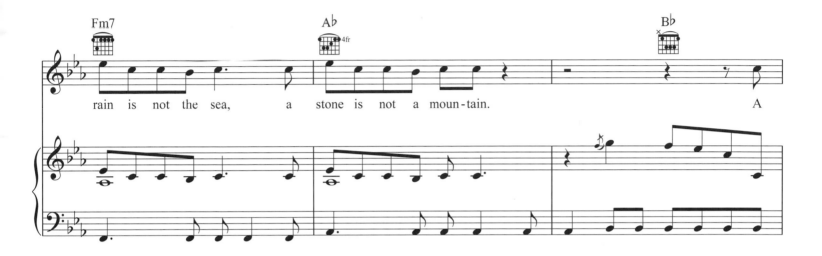

rain is not the sea, a stone is not a moun-tain. A

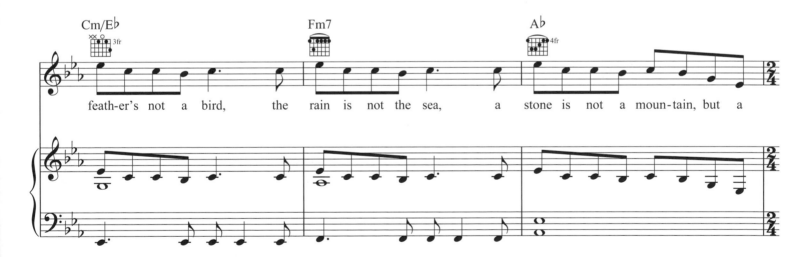

feath-er's not a bird, the rain is not the sea, a stone is not a moun-tain, but a

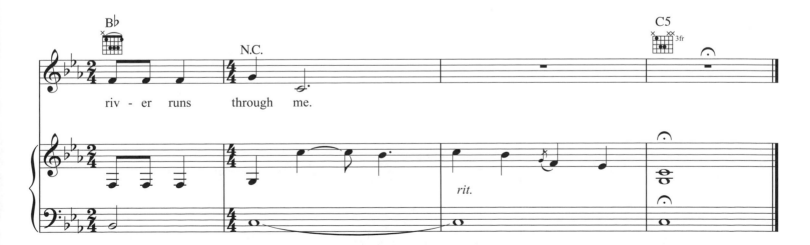

riv-er runs through me.

THE SUNKEN LANDS

Words and Music by ROSANNE CASH
and JOHN LEVENTHAL

Moderate shuffle

With pedal

Five cans of paint and the emp-ty fields
mud and tears melt the cot-ton bolls;

the dust re-veals.
it's a heav-y toll. Oh.

The chil-dren cry; the work nev-er ends.
His words are cruel, and they sting like fire,

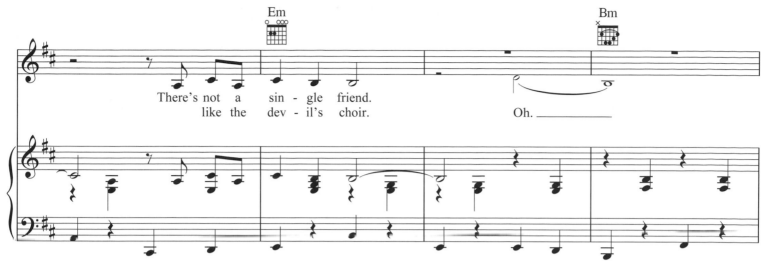

There's not a sin - gle friend.
like the dev - il's choir.

Oh. _____

Who will hold _ her hand in the sunk - en
But who will hold _ her hand in the sunk - en

lands?
lands?

work   is   done _____ in the sunk-en lands. _   There's five

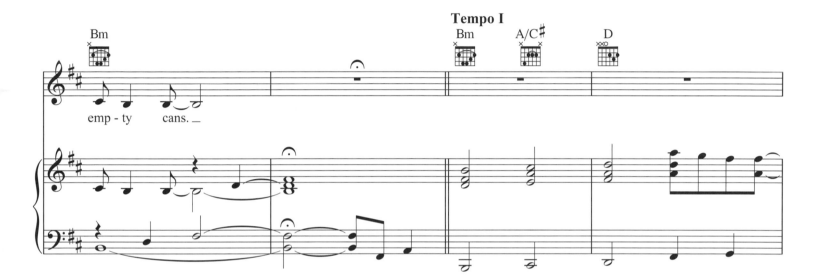

emp-ty   cans. _

ETTA'S TUNE

Words and Music by ROSANNE CASH
and JOHN LEVENTHAL

Moderately

With pedal

"What's the tem-p'ra-ture, dar - ling?" _ "A hun-dred or more." _

_ The horse is paw - ing at _____ the dust; _ vio - lets

wilt - ing by the door. _____ But you pour your strong - est cof -

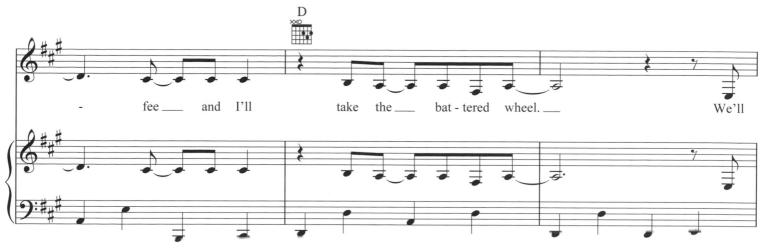

fee ___ and I'll take the ___ bat - tered wheel. ___ We'll

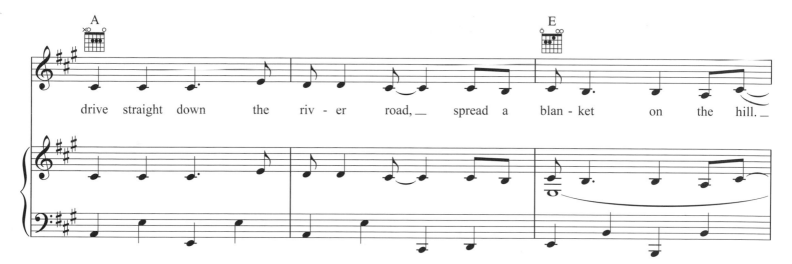

drive straight down the riv - er road, ___ spread a blan - ket on the hill. ___

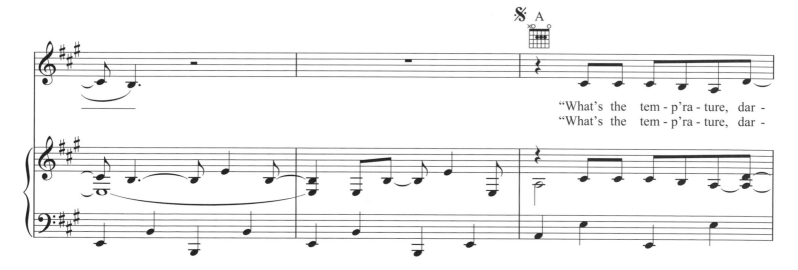

"What's the tem - p'ra - ture, dar -
"What's the tem - p'ra - ture, dar -

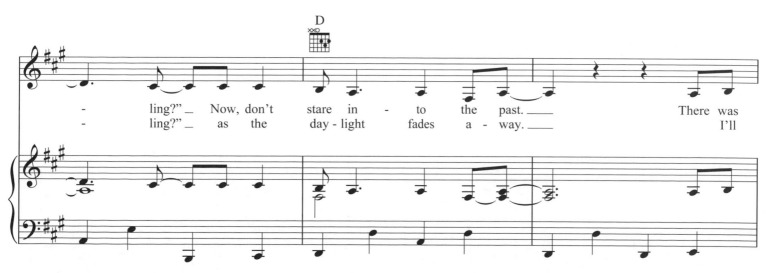

- ling?" ___ Now, don't stare in - to the past. ___ There was
- ling?" ___ as the day - light fades a - way. ___ I'll

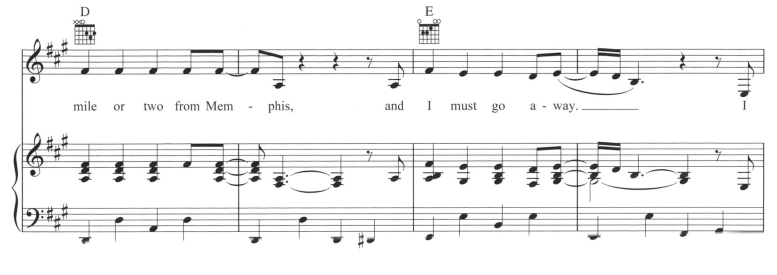

mile or two from Mem - phis, and I must go a - way._____ I

tore up all the high - ways, { now there's noth-ing left to say.___ }
{ there's noth-ing left to say.___ }

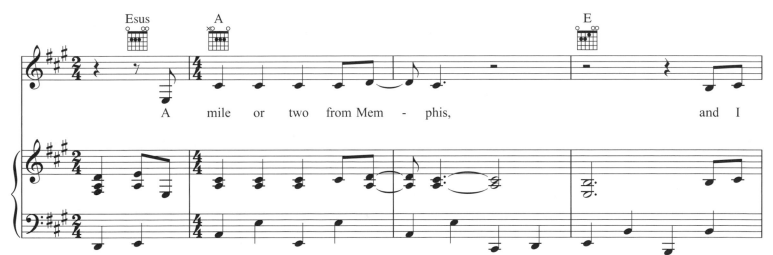

A mile or two from Mem - phis, and I

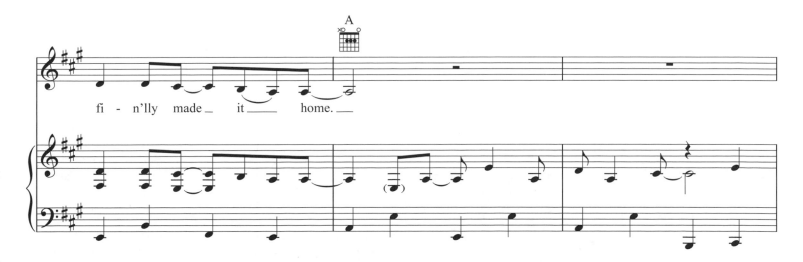

fi - n'lly made__ it___ home.__

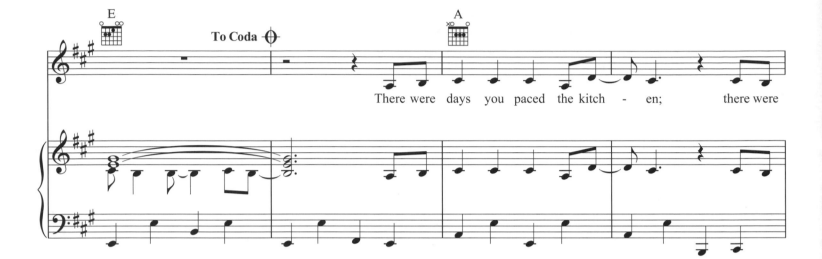

There were days you paced the kitch - en; there were

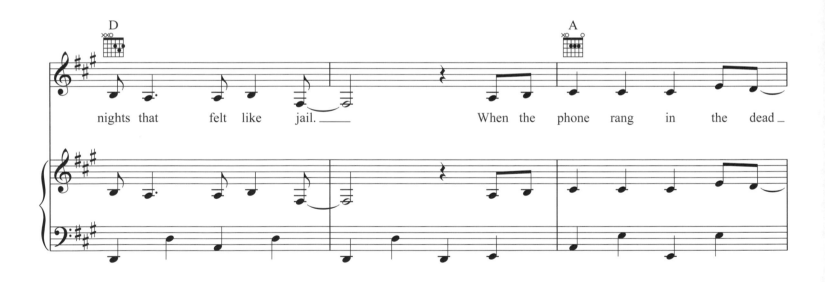

nights that felt like jail. _____ When the phone rang in the dead _

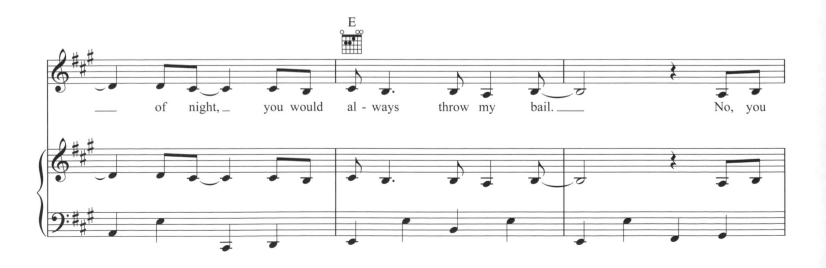

_____ of night, _ you would al - ways throw my bail. _____ No, you

never touched the whis - key, and you nev - er took the pills. ___

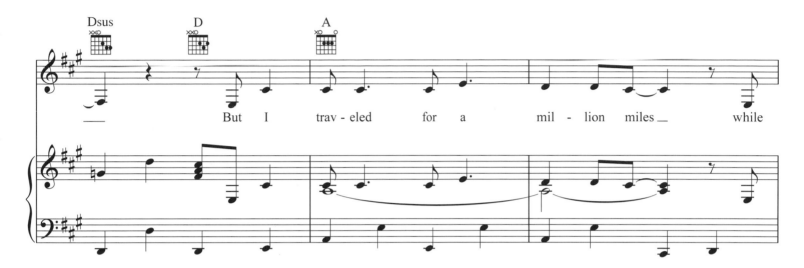

___ But I trav - eled for a mil - lion miles ___ while

D.S. al Coda

you were stand - ing still. ___

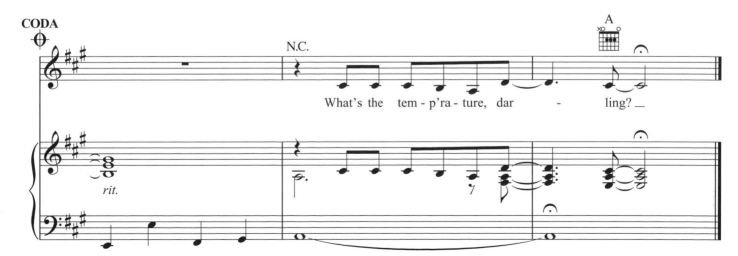

CODA

N.C.

What's the tem - p'ra - ture, dar - ling? ___

rit.

MODERN BLUE

Words and Music by ROSANNE CASH
and JOHN LEVENTHAL

* Recorded a half step lower.

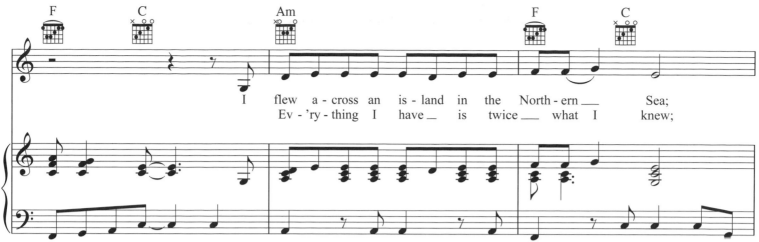

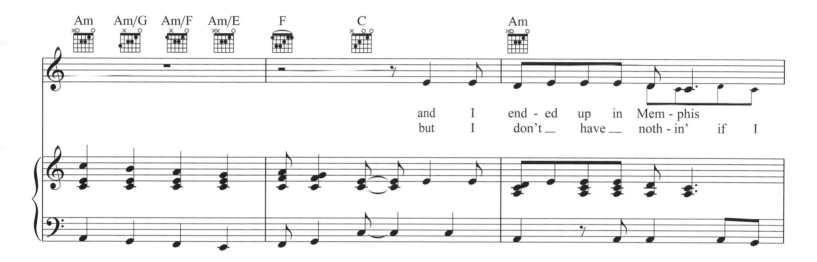

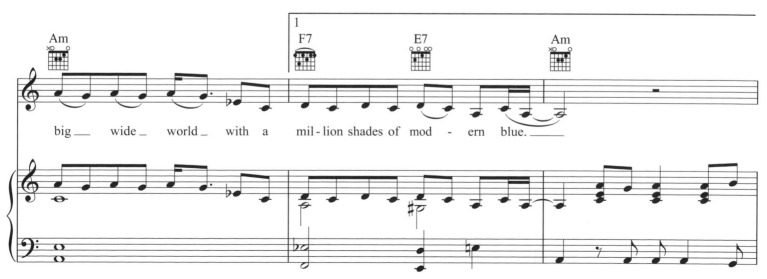

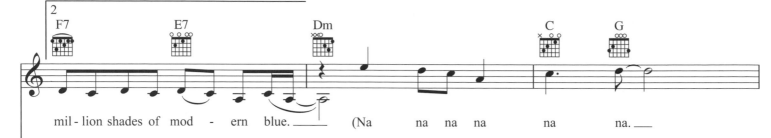

mil - lion shades of mod - ern blue. _____ (Na na na na na na. ___

Na na na na na na. _____ Na na na na.)

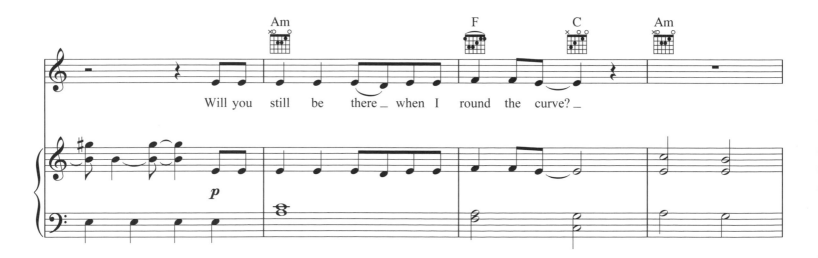

Will you still be there _ when I round the curve? _

Will you hold my hand _ when I lose _ my nerve? _

Oh, _ I went to Bar - ce - lo - na, and my mind got changed;

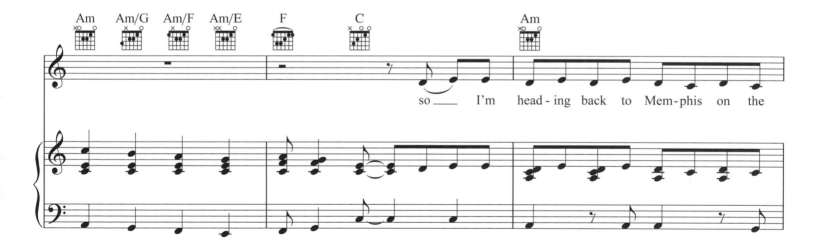

so _ I'm head - ing back to Mem - phis on the

mid - night train. _ I keep my head down; _ I keep my eyes on you. It's a

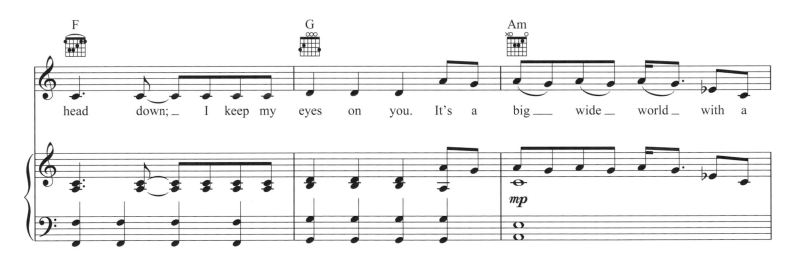

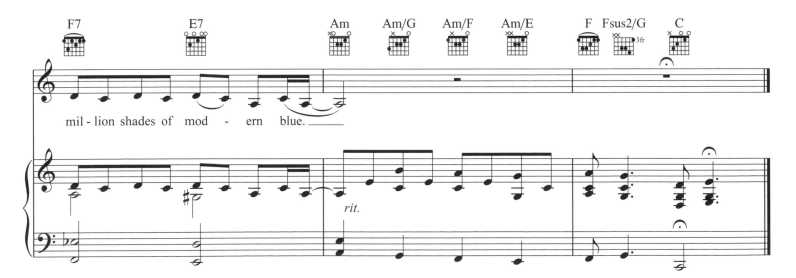

TELL HEAVEN

Words and Music by ROSANNE CASH
and JOHN LEVENTHAL

Moderately slow

mp

With pedal

1. When you're like a bro - ken bird, __ tell Heav - en; __
2. *Instrumental solo*

bat - tered wings a - gainst __ a dark - ened day. __

When your wor - ries won't let you sleep, __ tell Heav -

-en.

When the tears won't ev - er go _____ a - way. _____

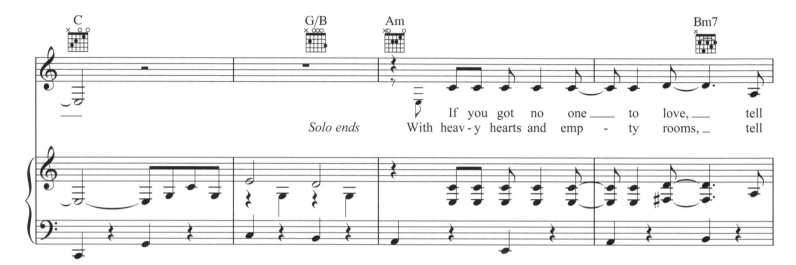

_____

Solo ends

If you got no one _____ to love, _____ tell

With heav - y hearts and emp - ty rooms, _____ tell

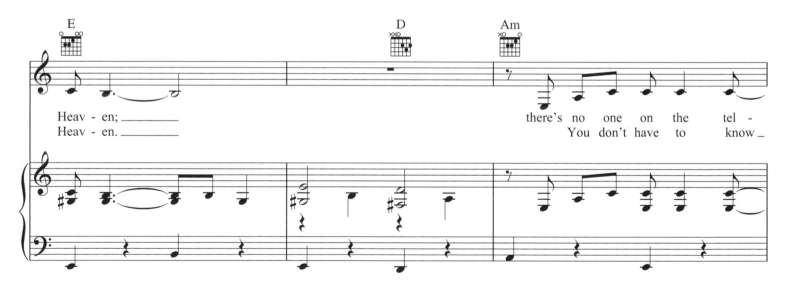

Heav - en; _____

Heav - en. _____

there's no one on the tel -

You don't have to know _____

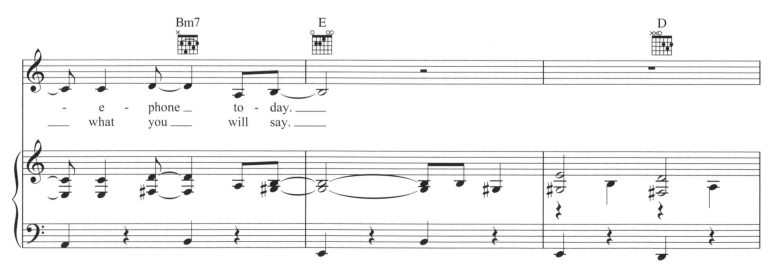

- e - phone _____ to - day. _____

_____ what you _____ will say. _____

When ev-'ry sto-ry falls _____ a - part, _____ tell Heav - en; _____
The emp-ty sky may nev - er take _____ our bur - dens; _____

noth - ing good seems like _____ it - 'll come _____ your
some-thing good will some - day _____ come _____ our

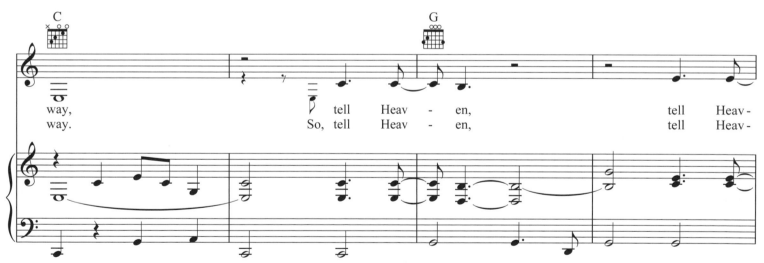

way, tell Heav - en, tell Heav-
way. So, tell Heav - en, tell Heav-

- en.
- en. _____

THE LONG WAY HOME

Words and Music by ROSANNE CASH
and JOHN LEVENTHAL

WORLD OF STRANGE DESIGN

Words and Music by ROSANNE CASH
and JOHN LEVENTHAL

Well, you're

not from a - round ___ here, you're prob - 'ly not ___ our
like to have the o - cean, but I set - tled for ___ the
talk a - bout your ___ drink - ing, but not a - bout ___ your

kind. It's hot from March ___ to Christ - mas, and
rain. I hum - bly asked ___ for true ___ love, there was
thirst. You set off through ___ the mine ___ field like

oth - er things _ you'll find
such a price _ to find pay.
you were round - ing first.

won't fit your old _ i -
'Cause this room was filled _ with
So o - pen up _ a

de - as: they're a line in shift - ing sands. You'll
trou - ble and _ sac - ra - ments de - ceived: now
win - dow and hand the ba - by through.

walk a - cross _ a ghost - ly bridge _ to a crum - bling prom - ised land. _
I'm a jew - el in _ the shade _ of his weep - ing wil - low tree. _
Point her towards _ the ghost - ly bridge, _ and _ she'll know what to do. _

C/E   F5

If Je - sus came _ from Mis - sis - sip - pi, _

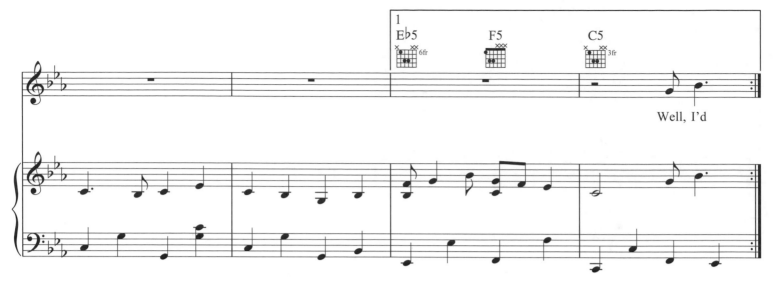

Well, I'd

Guitar solo ad lib.

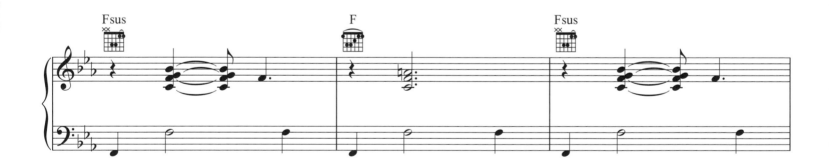

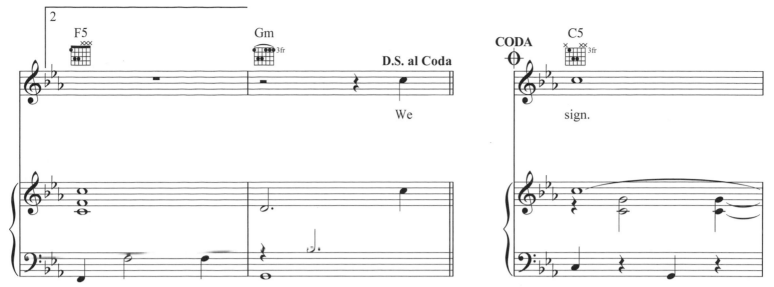

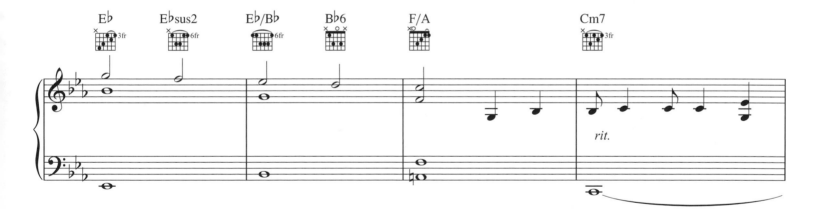

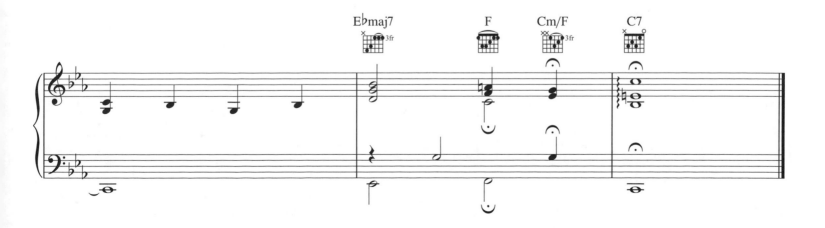

NIGHT SCHOOL

Words and Music by ROSANNE CASH
and JOHN LEVENTHAL

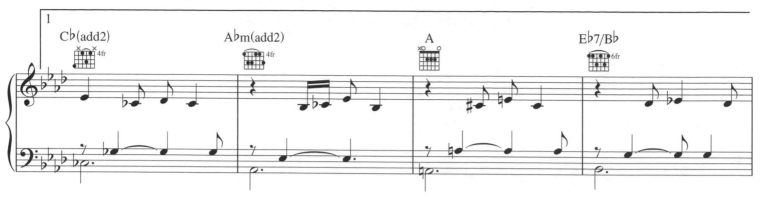

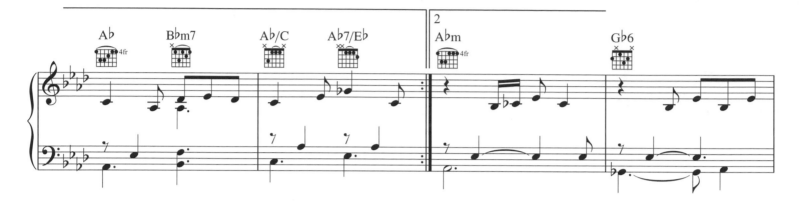

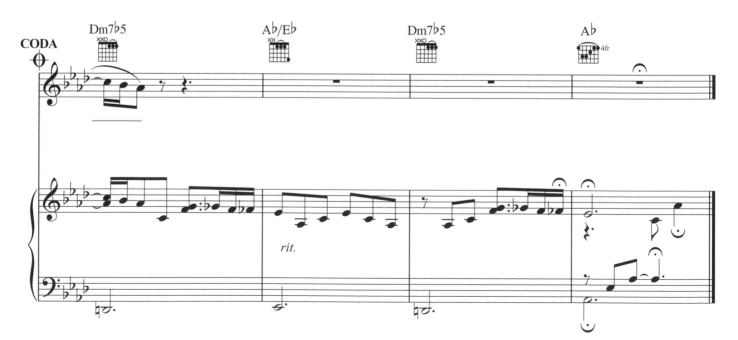

50,000 WATTS

Words and Music by ROSANNE CASH
and JOHN LEVENTHAL

WHEN THE MASTER CALLS THE ROLL

Words and Music by ROSANNE CASH,
JOHN LEVENTHAL and RODNEY CROWELL

Acoustic Folk

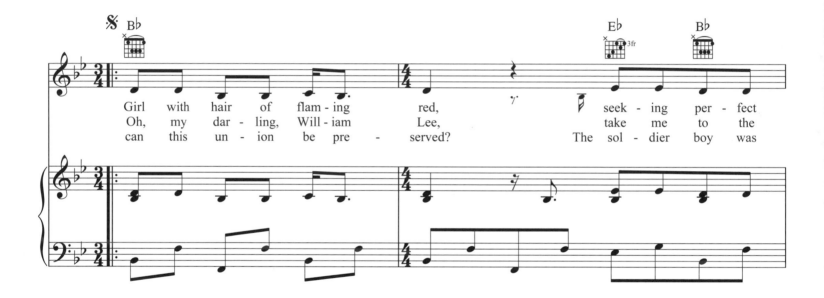

Girl with hair of flam - ing red,   seek - ing per - fect
Oh, my dar - ling, Will - iam Lee,   take me to the
can this un - ion be pre - served?   The sol - dier boy was

lov - er.   For to lie ____ down on her feath - er bed, ___
al - tar.   I don't have strength ___ to watch you as you leave ___
cry - ing.   I will nev - er tra - vel back to her ___

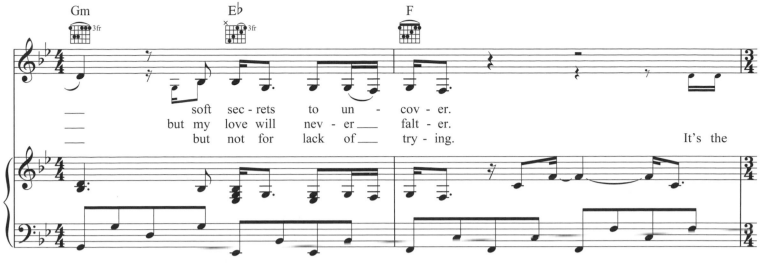

soft sec - rets to un - cov - er.
but my love will nev - er ___ falt - er.
but not for lack of ___ try - ing. It's the

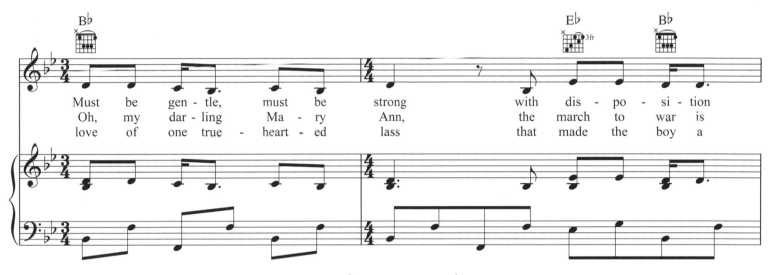

Must be gen - tle, must be strong with dis - po - si - tion
Oh, my dar - ling Ma - ry Ann, the march to war is
love of one true - heart - ed lass that made the boy a

sun - ny. Just as faith - ful as ___ the day ___ is
call - ing. Some - where far a - cross ___ these South - ern
he - ro. But a ri - fle ball ___ and a can - non

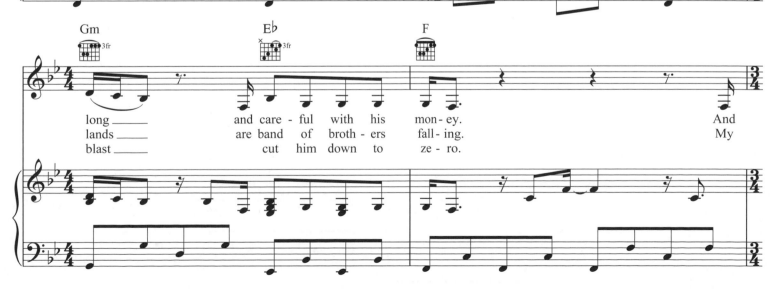

long ___ and care - ful with his mon - ey. And
lands ___ are band of broth - ers fall - ing. My
blast ___ cut him down to ze - ro.

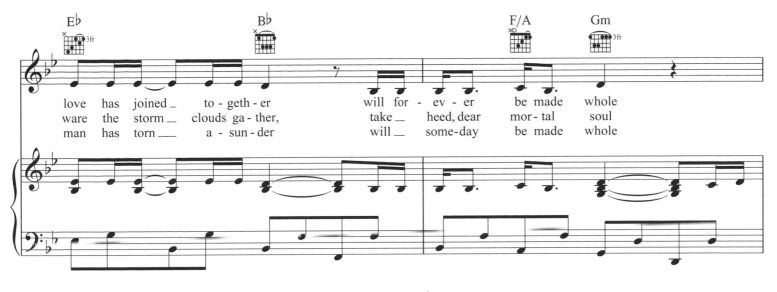

love has joined __ to-geth-er   will for - ev - er   be made   whole
ware the storm __ clouds ga - ther,   take __ heed, dear   mor - tal   soul
man has torn __ a - sun - der   will __ some-day   be made   whole

when the mas - ter calls __ the roll. ____
when the mas - ter calls __ the roll. ____
when the mas - ter calls __

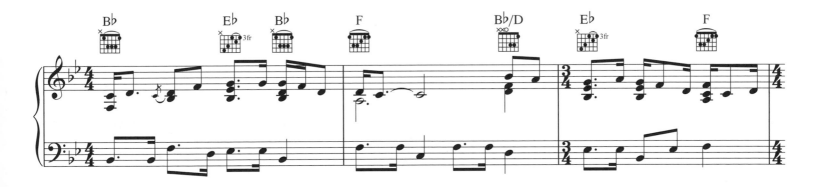

But

CODA

the roll. Though the storm clouds ga - ther, let the

un - ion be made whole when the mas - ter calls __

the roll. __

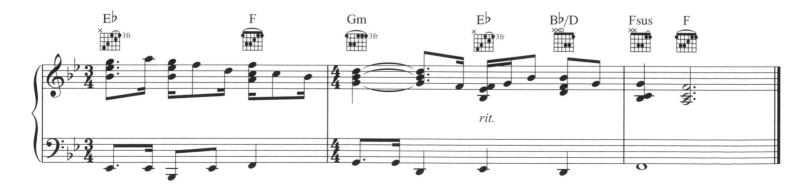

rit.

MONEY ROAD

Words and Music by ROSANNE CASH
and JOHN LEVENTHAL

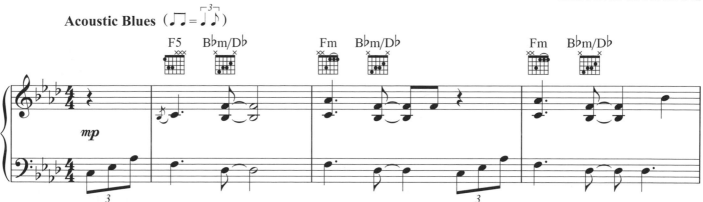

I was dream-ing a-bout ___ the Tal - la-hatch-ie Bridge. ___
lone - some ___ boy ___ in a for-eign ___ land. ___
dream-ing a-bout ___ the ___ deep-est ___ blue. ___

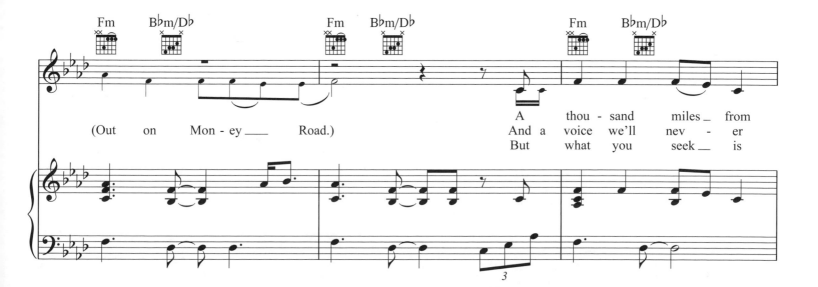

(Out on Mon-ey ___ Road.)
A thou-sand miles ___ from
And a voice we'll nev - er
But what you seek ___ is

where we live. _____
un - der - stand. _____ (Out on ___ Mon - ey ___ Road.) ___
seek - ing you. _____

But the
You can

long line at the pearl - y gate, ___ the keep - ers of our
One lies in the Zi - on yard ___ and one sleeps on the
cross the bridge and carve ___ your name ___ but the riv - er stays the

fate. None of them ___ will con - gre - gate _____ out ___
riv - er bar. _____ Nei - ther one ___ got ver - y far _____ out ___
same. _____ We left but nev - er went a - way, _____ out ___

To Coda

1

___ on Mon - ey ___ Road. ___

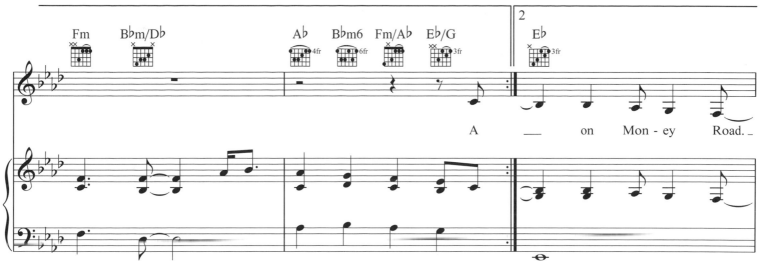

A ___ on Mon - ey Road. ___

Out ___ on ___ Mon - ey Road. ___

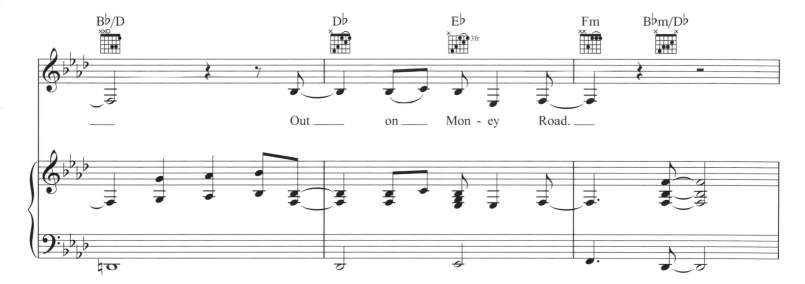

Guitar solo ad lib.

I was

D.S. al Coda

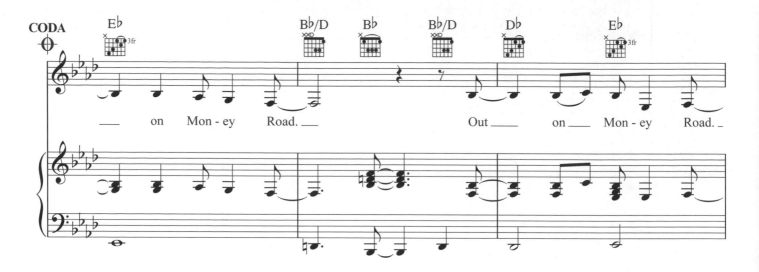

on Mon-ey Road. Out on Mon-ey Road.

Out on Mon-ey Road, out on Mon-ey Road.

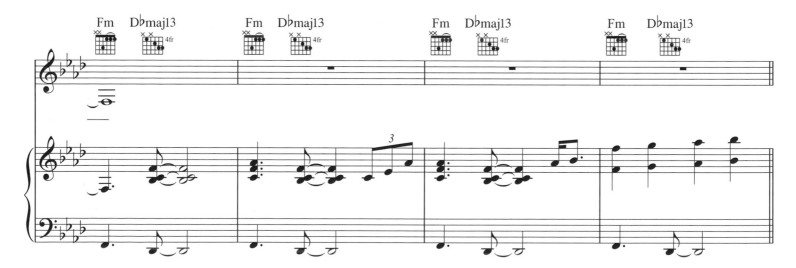

Repeat ad lib. and Fade | **Optional Ending**

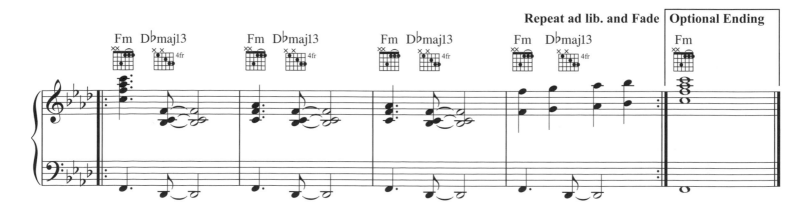